CYMR
WRTH
FEDDWI

*Learn Welsh While You get P*ssed!*

Stephen Owen Rule

Hunan-gyhoeddwyd gyda hawlfraint
© 2022 gan Stephen Rule

Cedwir pob hawl. Ni chaniateir ailgyhoeddi neu ddefnyddio unrhyw ran o'r llyfr hwn mewn unrhyw fodd heb ganiatâd perchennog yr hawlfraint ar wahân i ddyfyniadau mewn adolygiad llyfr. Am ragor o wybodaeth, cyfeiriad e-bost: stecymru14@gmail.com.

Argraffiad llyfr / e-lyfr cyntaf: Hydref 2022

ISBN: 9798353362296

Dyluniad y clawr gan Stephen Rule

Self-published and copyrighted
© 2022 by Stephen Rule

All rights reserved. No part of this book may be reproduced or used in any manner without written permission of the copyright owner except for the use of quotations in a book review. For more information, email address: stecymru14@gmail.com.

First paperback / e-book edition: October 2022

ISBN: 9798353362296

Cover design by Stephen Rule

Doctor Cymraeg

Gorau Dysgu Cyd Ddysgu

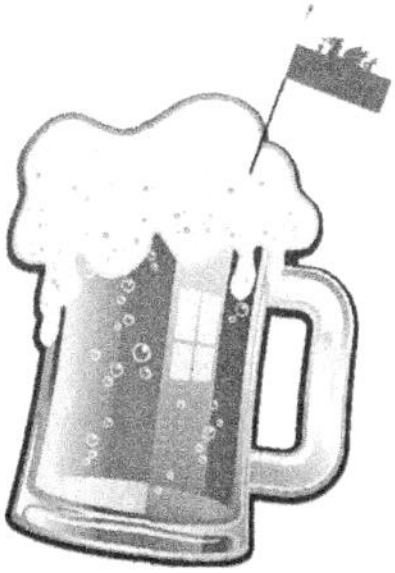

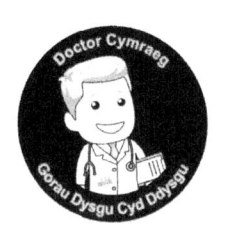

CYMRAEG WRTH FEDDWI
*Learn Welsh While You Get P*ssed*

Following the insane (and totally unexpected) success of my first book in the 'Welsh While You...' series*, *Welsh While You Bonk* (ISBN: 9798422469628), it became inevitable that I'd have to put something else similar together. With comments such as "If this doesn't get people into learning Welsh, I don't know what will," smattered with mutterings of "Welsh While You Bonk? You've definitely peaked too soon!" (Coincidentally, a phrase I now regret not included in the first book!), I yearned for months for a new idea to get folk giggling while they picked up some more phrases (and grammar tips) in our wonderful language.

As a former learner of Welsh myself, I'm often asked to recall the first moments and occasions when I initially admitted fluency. As it happens, those memories hark back to the pub when, with some Dutch courage flowing through me, I felt no fear in sharing the Welsh I knew... howsoever hazy those memories are, for obvious reasons!

DISCLAIMER: I was tempted to leave the following message unsaid as I often find learners of Welsh to be rather level-headed folk, but, having witnessed first-hand what devastation alcohol can yield, please drink responsibly. Diolch.

As with Welsh While You Bonk, the 30 phrases herein are distributed into three sections; *Before* (ie getting ready to hit the tiles), *During* (ie phrases for when one is consuming the devil's nectar), and *After* (ie when one inevitable must reach for the flat cola and greasy fry-up). Each section consists of 10 phrases you can use in almost all situations where alcohol is involved, plus notes on how the phrases can be modified for use in less drunken circumstances.

Right, fetch me a cold Wrecsam Lager and let's get on it!

* it wasn't supposed to be a series!

CYN
Before

Ffansïo mynd am beint?

Fancy going for a pint?

Ffansïo has been sneakily robbed from English like the swig of your mate's pint you take while they're not looking. As it's a verb, we can add **-io** at the end without sounding like an idiot trying to lazily make any word 'sound Welsh'. There are plenty of examples too; **parcio** (= *to park*), **marcio** (= *to mark*), **lyfio** (= *to love*), **licio** (= *to like*), **dreifio** (= *to drive*), etc.

'*For*' can be a tough one to translate into Welsh – not least because prepositions don't always equate to the same word in English. **Am**, which can also mean '*at [a time]*' or '*about*' is used for '*for*' here. Other words for '*for*' include '**i**' and '**ar gyfer**,'... but you'll have to come for a slurp with me if you want a more full explanation of how and when they're used. Notice, too, how **am** causes a soft mutation on the following word. This is always the case.

Iawn, ond 'mond un bach sydyn

Alright, but only a [little] quick one

'Mond possesses an apostrophe before it because it's actually a contraction of **dim ond**, which translates literally as *nothing/nought but*. The other term for *only* in Welsh is **yn unig**, but I tend to reserve this for the end of clauses or sentences > **'On i 'mond isio un** vs **'On i isio un yn unig** (= *I only wanted one, I was only wanting one*).

The term **bach** is common knowledge to anyone who's been exposed to Welsh in any school setting. Translating as *'small'*, *'little,'* it's often thrown into Welsh sentences where, in English, one might often omit it; **mae hi'n un bach ddel** > *She's a [little] pretty one*.

Sydyn is a direct lifting from the English word *'sudden.'* It's become more and more popular in Welsh versus the term **cyflym** (= *fast, quick*); **Tria fod yn sydyn, 'nei di?** (= *Try to be quick, will ya?*).

Allan am sesh heno?

Out for a sesh tonight?

For the southern drinkers out there, there's a big chance you'll have stumbled across (pun intended!) **ma's** as the word for *out*. Although **allan** has become the modern language's standard form for it, looking at Cornish (**yn-mes**) and Breton (**er-maez**) – deriving from '**i'r maes**' (*to the field*) – clearly demand **ma's** should be getting a bit more respect. But this is my book and I'm from the north east, so deal with it.

Sesh is clearly a borrowing from English; with many speakers referring to a night on the loopy juice as a '*session.*' I must admit, **sesh** was a word I heard far more in Welsh-speaking circles than I ever heard '*session*' (and any variation of it) when around English speakers.

Dw i 'di bwcio tacsi yn barod

*I've booked
A taxi already*

Here's another good time to explain what's happening with **'di**. The perfect particle '**wedi**' is used to form the perfect tense in Welsh. It equates to 'have/has [done something]' in English; for example, **mae hi wedi bod** = *she has been*, **'swn i wedi mynd** = *I would have gone*. When teaching Welsh I often bring students' attentions to the other occasion where **wedi** is used – in telling the time. **Wedi** here means '*past*', and this can help learners a lot when forming the perfect tense; **dw i <u>wedi</u> siarad** > *I am <u>past</u> speaking* > *I <u>have</u> spoke<u>n</u>*. Get it? In this example, wedi has been contracted to **'di** – a rather common occurence in the spoken language.

Parod (*ready*) is a pretty versatile to be honest. It can be used as an adjective to describe something *ready*; **arian parod** = *ready money* = *cash*. It can be used in questions like '**wyt ti'n barod?**' (*are you ready?*). And it can be used as an adverb by fronting it with **yn** and mutating softly; = *already/readily*.

Blaen-ddiodydd yn tŷ fi, 'te?

Pre-drinks at mine, then?

Ok, so the reason you can't locate **blaen-ddiodydd** in your dictionary is because I just made it up. But that's the cool thing about Welsh; because it was originally an analytical language, we can pretty much shove any two words together to create new ones.

Blaengroen = *Foreskin*. Not sure why that was the word that came to my headfirst! I'd best think of another one quickly... what about **blaendal** = *deposit*?... where **tâl** is a '*payment*'.

Notice how the *Tesco Value* way of expressing possession has been used here. The 'purists' amongst you will prefer using **fy + tŷ** and adding a nasal mutation to form **fy nhŷ**. As beautiful as this is, it's far more common with the younger folk to just chuck the pronoun after the noun. It avoids the need for those nasty mutations, and it follows the pattern of showing possession when using any noun; **tŷ Nain** = *Grandma's house*, **Tŷ pawb** = *Everyone's house*, etc.

'**Te** derives from **ynte** meaning '*then*'. You might also hear '**ta** in north Wales, '**de** in south Wales, and **[fe]lly** (= *so, therefore*) in north-west Wales.

Faint o'r gloch awn ni heno?

What time will we go tonight?

If you've had any sort of education in Wales or have studied Welsh to even the smallest degree, **faint o'r gloch?** is probably a phrase with which you're rather familiar. What people don't tend to realise is that it's actually asking '*how many of the clock?*' – a throwback to when one would ask how many times the hourly village church bells had rung. This is also why we answer the question with '**X o'r gloch**' (*X of the clock*), coincidentally the same sentiment for why '*X o'clock*' is uttered in English.

Awn ni, on the other hand, isn't quite so common unless you've been lucky enough to have had some sort of Welsh-speaking background/exposure. Grammatically described as the present/future tense first person plural of the verbal noun, '**mynd**,' **awn ni** literally equates to '*we [will] go*' in English. What's cool about the Welsh version, however, is how it can suggest '*let's go*' too. On top of that, it doesn't need to change at all to form a question (**awn ni heno?** = *shall we go tonight?*) and only needs a **ddim** after it to form the negative (**awn ni ddim yna** = *we won't go there*).

Ti'n gw'bod pwy sy'n dod?

Do you know who's coming?

Gwybod – meaning *'to know [something]'* – is shortened a lot in Welsh; all variations of which are common and therefore very useful to... erm... *know*! See what I did there? Regional differences include; **gw'bod, gw'bo', gwŷbod**, as well as phrases such as **sai'mo** (= *I dunno*), **dwm'bo** (= *I dunno*), **ti'(n)gw'bo'?** (= *Ya know?*).

You might have been told that **sy'n** is enough to express *'who is/are'* (and also *'that is/are'* and *'which is/are'*), with many learners still putting in **pwy** (= *who*) when it's not strictly needed. Aside from the fact you shouldn't ever worry about including it, the sentence above represents one of the only occasions when you actually do need **pwy** before **sy'n**... when you're asking a question. Check these out for a better explanation; **Pwy sy'n siarad?** (= *Who's talking?*) vs **Owen <u>sy'n</u> siarad** (= *it's Owen <u>who is</u> talking*). I need a lie down!

Dim sambûca tro 'ma!

No sambuca this time!

Obviously, you can demand that you're exempt from any alcoholic beverage you like – I'm just using this one because I still haven't been able to stomach the stuff since I was in a bar at 19-years-old and managed to fill a table with empty 10+ empty shot glasses and some vomit!

Perhaps you're chuckling at the way I've used the very-Welsh **ŵ** to express the sound '*oo*'. This is quite common in loaned words, to be fair; for example, **cŵl** = *cool*, **sbŵci** = *spooky*, **grŵp** = *group*, **bambŵ** = *bamboo*, **cangarŵ** = *kangaroo*, etc.

Dare I say it, you're probably rather annoyed that '*time*' has been translated as **tro** here, rather than **amser**. **Amser** relates to the concept of *time*; i.e., the thing you ask for when organising a night out, or the thing there's not enough of when your mates want to move on to the next bar and you've still got half a pint left!

Tro, on the other hand, relates more to '*an occasion*' and can be seen/heard in instances such as **am y tro** (= *for now*), **dros dro** (= *temporar(il)y*), and **tro ar ôl tro** (= *time after time*).

Methu aros i gael hwyl

Can't wait to have [some] fun

Methu is one of my favourite verbs in Welsh. Yes, I have favourite verbs... leave me alone!

Strictly equating to '*to fail*', **methu** is used nowadays to express '*cannot*,' which, for me, has always seemed a little more optimistic a thing to say; *failing* at doing something being less 'final' than saying you *cannot* do it. **Dw i methu dod** = *I can't come*, **Oedd o methu credu o** = *He couldn't believe it/him*.

In southern dialects you'll also hear/see **ffaeli** and **ffili**; both of which are borrowings from the word '*fail*' itself.

Finally, a quick nod to '**i**' – which equates to '*to*' or '*for*' in Welsh – seen here causing a soft mutation. This, as with most other prepositions in Welsh, is always the case.

Dw i'n meddwl bod 'na fand yn y dafarn hefyd

I think there's a band in the pub too

With or without the **'na** part, you might already know that **mae 'na** means *there is/are*. When used to join to clauses, or parts of sentences, we switch out **mae** for **bod** when we want to express '*that* there is/are'. One might also hear bod shortened to **bo'** (sounds like the English word '*bore*'), especially if people are trying to save even the tiniest moments for another swig of ale.

Notice, too, how the inclusion of (the actually unnecessary) **'na** causes a soft mutation; **mae band** vs **mae 'na fand** – both meaning *there's a band*.

Fun fact; some people treat **tafarn** (= *pub(lic house), inn, alehouse*) as a masculine word. Some nouns can be both... because Welsh is a pain-in-the-bottom sometimes! These include **tudalen** (= *(a) page*), **morfa** (= *(a) coastal marsh*), and **munud** (= *(a) minute*).

YN YSTOD
During

Dw i'n dechrau teimlo hwn

I'm starting to feel this [one]

A quick note on how Welsh deals with multiple verbs (or, strictly, verbal nouns) when arranged in a row like in this example. With only a few exceptions, we won't need '**i**' (= *to*) between verbs like English does. Essentially, we can say stuff like **dw i isio trïo mynd nofio** (= *I want to try to go to swim*). This is largely due to Welsh getting '*-ing*' for free; for example, **yfed** can equate to *drink*, *drinks*, and *drinking* in English.

Hwn is the pronoun equating to *this [one]* in English. Unfortunately, this is only the word for masculine stuff, with **hon** taking up the mantle for feminine things.

Although the common way of expressing *this [something]* can be formed by saying '**y [something] yma**,' the 'proper' way to do it is to use **hwn** or **hon** instead of **yma**. In addition to this becoming more and more rare in speech, you'll also need to know the gender of the *something* if you're going to use it; **y ci hwn** (= *this dog*) vs **y gath hon** (= *this cat*).

Ti byth yn dawnsio fel arfer!

You never usually dance!

For the purists readers, this sentence should indeed begin with **dwyt**, instead of just **ti**. I'm simply trying to use language how it's most likely to be heard in the wild here. But, if you did spot this, well played. I owe you a pint!

Byth is how we say *'never'* (and *'ever'* – but don't ask about that right now!) in Welsh. What I've always found cool about it is that it replaces **ddim** in sentences to make the sentiment it holds much stronger; for example, **dw i <u>ddim</u> yn hapus** (= *I'm <u>not</u> happy*) vs **dw i <u>byth</u> yn hapus** (= *I'm <u>never</u> happy*).

Fel arfer equates to both *'usually'* and *'as usual'* in Welsh... but they're effectively the same thing anyway, right?

The word '**arfer**' translates as *'(a) custom'* or *'(a) habit'* and can be found in phrases like '**yn ôl yr arfer**' (= *according to custom*). The word **ymarfer** (= *to practise, (a) practice, (an) exercise*) derives from **arfer**.

Dy rownd di ydy o

It's your round

Considering the construction of this phrase, you'll probably start to feel like you're sounding a bit like Yoda. You are – depending on how many pints you've quaffed – probably starting to look like him too!

Notice here how, because we're emphasising the fact that *it's <u>your</u> round*, we place it at the start of the sentence. We also do this when stating our names and/or occupations; **Stephen ydw i** (= *I'm Stephen*), **athro ydw i** (= *I'm a teacher*). English, in contrast, prefers to put stress on the word requiring emphasis in speech, or might use italics to show the same thing in writing. Welsh is all about the syntax!

Luckily, the fact that **dy** (= *your*) and **['rwyt] ti'n** (= *you're*) are so different to each other in Welsh, there's far less chance someone will think you're saying "*you're round*" rather than "*your round*" and you're in better stead to avoid a smack in the chops!

Ti 'di trïo Wrexham Lager eto?

Have you tried Wrexham Lager yet?

Once again – and as you'll hear in commonly in the wild – I've removed the **wyt** from the beginning of this sentence. You can pop it in if you like or keep your language nice and chavvy and omit it like I do.

As mentioned with an earlier phrase, **wedi** has once again been contracted to **'di** – something else rather common.

Something that's unfortunately <u>not</u> always common around Wales (outside the northeast, anyway) is answering **do, wrth gwrs!** (= *yes, of course!*) to this question. I should* add that other lagers are available, blah, blah, blah… but you won't want any others once you've got a good pint of Wrexham down your gills.

* This section is not sponsored by Wrexham Lager… but is most definitely supported by me!

'Sa' ti'n licio un arall?

Would you like another [one]?

The conditional (or past habitual) tense in Welsh can be confusing simply because there are so bloomin' many ways to express it! In north-west Wales you have **mi faswn i'n** (= *I would be*), in the north-east you have **byse'n** (= *it would be*), and southern dialects tend to punt for **fe fyddwn i'n** (= *I would be*)… not to mention '**pe bai'n**' and '**petaswn**' etc!

In this example, I've gone for what I say (and hear) most commonly. **'Sa' ti'n?** is short for **'Faset ti'n?** which means '*Would you (be)?*'

Nothing much more to say about **licio** other than, yes, it's stolen from '*like*' in English, and no, it's not as cool as **hoffi**.

Notice how we need the word **un** (= *one*) in this sentence, even though it's not really necessary in English. That's because **arall** is a pain and has to be accompanied by whatever it is of which your sentence needs *another*!

Gwna fo'n ddwbl...

*Make it
a double...*

Gwna is the imperative form of **gwneud** (= *to do, to make*). This means it's one of the most common ways we can command others to do or make something for us. **Gwna dy waith!** = *Do your work!*, **Gwna gacen iddyn nhw!** = *Make a cake for them!*, **Gwna hwnna, plîs!** = *Do that, please!*

If you fancy being a little more formal to the person behind the bar, swap out **gwna** for **gwnewch**.

There's no word for '*it*' in Welsh; much like quite a few other modern languages, of course. Instead, we use either **(f)o/(f)e** (= *him*) or **hi** (= *her*) depending on the gender of the noun to which '*it*' refers.

If you're ever unsure, most people tend to punt for the masculine one.

Pam does neb yn syrfio fi?

Why is no one serving me?

Neb is a great little word meaning *no one*. It's worth nothing here that double negatives *enhance* in Welsh, unlike in English where they cancel each other out. **Does neb yma** literally translates as *'there isn't no one here'* but is actually the correct way of expressing *'there's no one here'* or *'there isn't anyone here.'*

The frustration at not getting served at a bar even though you were definitely waiting before the last 5 people to get their drinks can be immense, but nothing compares to the frustration of being so intensely consumed trying to speak Welsh and thinking of every word when, the truth is, it's ok to shove an English word in there now and again...

Syrfio is clearly a borrowing from *'to serve'* (which is a verb, so adding **-io** is fine here), but purists would rather **gweini**. If you're reading Welsh, always say the word in your head; chances are you'll recognise the other words that, to the untrained eye, look like they're unequivocly Welsh but are actually just English terms in disguise, such as; **watshad** (= *to watch* > **gwylio**), **witshad** (= *to wait* > **aros**), **cwcio** (= *to cook* > **coginio**), **dreifio** (= to drive > **gyrru**), et al.

Paid mynd! Arhosa am un arall!

Don't go! Stay for one more!

Paid is how we express '*don't*' in Welsh and can be a really useful term. **Paid mynd yna!** (= *don't go there!*), **paid siarad efo neb!** (= *don't speak to anyone!*), **paid b'yta hwnna!** (= *don't eat that!*). You'll also see **paid** [correctly] used with an **â** following it. Also note the formal/plural form; **peidiwch** [â].

The keen eye will spot a few interesting points regarding the word **arhosa**. The word is built from **aros** (= *to stay*, *to wait*) with the singular imperative ending **-a**, which turns **aros** into somewhat of a command. The reason for the additional **-h-** is due to where the accent in the word lies. You'll find this happen when morphemes are affixed to other words like **cynnwys** (= *to contain, to include*) > **cynhwysion** (= *contents*).

Although **mwy** is the most common term for '*more*' in Welsh, when expressing phrases like '*one more*', Welsh uses the word '**arall**' (= *[an]other*). **Un arall** literally translates as '*another one*', which is just as correct in English as using '*one more.*'

Lle awn ni nesa'?

Where shall we go next?

Notice here how I'm using **lle** as the question word, *where*. This is generally a northern thing to do, with southerners (and English-medium schools across the whole of the country teaching Welsh) preferring **ble**. There is a spot for **lle** in formal language, mind... **lle** is the noun '*[a] place.*'

As I talked about **awn ni** earlier, I won't go into detail to explain it again. Instead, I'll show you the breakdown of it for each person... because, why not?;

af (i) = *I'll go, I go*
ei (di) = *you'll go, you go*
eith (o)/aiff (e)* = *he'll go, he goes*
eith/aiff (hi)* = *she'll go, she goes*
awn (ni) = *we'll go, we go*
ewch (chi) = *you'll go, you go*
ân (nhw) = *they'll go, they go*

> * **â ef/hi** is the super posh version that you definitely won't hear in many Welsh boozers!

Be' am wydriad o ddŵr yn lle?

What about a glass of water instead?

Looking after your buddies is imperative on a night out and knowing when to rehydrate is up there with holding your girlfriend's hair while they get up close and personal with a toilet seat.

Check a dictionary and you'll find that *glass* is **gwydr**, but it wouldn't be Welsh if there weren't exceptions. **Gwydr** refers to the material used to make something like a window or the bottom of a posh boat, where as **gwydriad** is the word we use for the vessels that hold a beverage. If, even after a couple yourself, this is still too confusing, you could always change out the '**wydraid o**' part for '**yfed**' (= *drinking*), or just remove it completely.

When studying for my A-levels – and before you ask, this is not a confession of me drinking underage – I remember my speaking assessment like it was yesterday. One particular part that stands out is asking the examiner how to say '*instead [of]*', and him then explaining how we instead say '*in place [of]*' via **yn lle**. Cool, huh?

AR ÔL
After

Mae fy mhen i fatha troed!

My head's like a foot!

For those hoping to find beautiful and authentic Welsh idioms that the natives use, I'm afraid you're in the wrong place! But don't feel as let down as the person in your group whose favourite 'famous last words' are "I can carry 4 pints... don't worry!", this is still a funny phrase to use while nursing the hangover from hell!

For those following mutations closely, **fy** (= *my*) causes a nasal mutation; **p** > **mh**. **Fy** can often be dropped in speech yielding, in this instance, **mae 'mhen i**. People do this because **fy** is the only personal pronoun that causes the nasal mutation, so, as soon as the counterpart hears **'mhen** rather than **pen**, they know exactly whose *head* is being discussed.

Fatha is super common up north and is used instead of **fel** (= *such (as), like*). I've got a feeling that **fatha** derives from '**fath o**' which means '*type/sort/kind of*', but you'll have to ask someone better qualified – like the Doctor Cymraeg – to confirm that for you!

Sawl paracetamol ga' i mewn un diwrnod?

How many paracetamol can I have in one day?

Learners of Welsh are far more likely to have encountered **faint** as '*how much*' or '*how many*,' but **sawl** is also used. As a rule of thumb, **faint (o)** comes before a softly-mutated plural noun, and **sawl** precedes a singular noun; for example, **faint o ddiodydd?** vs **sawl diod?**

Sawl can also be used as a noun to express '*a number of*'; for example, **mae gen i sawl diod yn fy llaw** = *I've got a number of drinks in my hand*.

I bet you're well accustomed to seeing '**ga' i?**' – especially if you've either had a full bladder in school or been brave enough to order a beer at a pub in Wales. Deriving from **cael** (= *to get, to be allowed*), **ca' i?** or **ga' i?** actually translate as '*will I get?*' or '*will I be allowed?*'

Don't think that it can't be used in positions other than at the beginning of sentences or questions... **Pryd ga' i brynu diod i ti?** = *When may I buy a beer for you?*, **Dw i ddim yn siŵr os ga' i weld yn iawn** = *I'm not sure if <u>I can</u> see well*.

Dw i'm yn cofio'm byd!

I don't remember anything!

D(d)im, in speech, is often shortened to **'m**. **Dw i'm yn** (= *I'm not, I don't*) is a shortening of **dw i ddim yn**, **'sgenai'm** (= *I haven't got (a/any)*) comes from **does gen' i ddim**. In this instance it might be tough to spot/hear out in the wild... especially if you've got a bit of the devil's nectar in your gills. All I can do is promise that the more you expose yourself to Welsh, the more your brain will start to take it in and understand it naturally.

The actual phrase used here is **dim byd**. Actually translating as *'no world,'* it's how we express *'absolutely nothing'*, or I guess we could look at it as *'nothing in the world.'*

Do!?

Did I?

You'll often find this little beauty accompanied by a look of total confusion and impending doom, embarrassment, or both. We've all been there!

Do – pronounced as the English word 'door' – is used to answer '*yes*' to questions in the past tense; "**Est ti adre' ar ôl y gêm?**" "**Do**" (= *Did you go home after the game? Yes, I did*). No matter the person, the answer remains the same; "**Wnaeth o'i waith cartref?**" "**Do**" (= *Did he do his homework? Yes, he did*).

In north Wales, it's also used when asked a question in the perfect tense where southern dialects would answer with '**ydw; ydy**'. "**Wyt ti wedi gweld hwnna?**" "**Do**" (= *Have you seen that? Yes, I have*).

The negative version is **naddo**.

Be' oedd enw ti eto?

What was your name again?

Stephen... my name's Stephen. I also answer to 'Doctor Cymraeg,' 'Twpsyn,' and 'Oi, you!.'

One thing that's important you <u>don't</u> let slip your mind – no matter how much the hangover is taking its grip – is that, despite using the common '**be'**' here for '*what*', the standard (and just-as-common) term for it is '**beth**.'

Fun fact:- the question word '**beth**' comes from '**pa beth**' which translates literally to '*which thing?*' You'll see similar derivations with **ble** (= *where*) < **pa le** (= *which place*), **pwy** (= *who(m)*) < **pa hwy** (= *which [of] them*), **pryd** (= *when*) < **pa bryd** (= *[at] which time*), and **pam** (= *why*) < **paham / pa ham** (= *which reason*).

Finally, **eto** means '*again*', but it's also used to express '*yet*.' Unfortunately, the term '*yet again*' is '**unwaith eto**' in Welsh – literally, *once again* – which, for me, is a massive missed opportunity!

Dim gwely fi ydi hwn!

This isn't my bed!

The hilariousness of this sentence is that there's definitely someone out there who's experienced this. I haven't... I promise.

The sentence construction here can often throw learners of Welsh and is one that took me a while to figure out when I was learning. The problem is, it's both a common and extremely useful thing to be able to express that something isn't yours. Noticing how *'not my bed is this'* is the construction – ie prioritising the subject/noun of the sentence rather than shoving it at the end, like in English – will hopefully help you understand this little Welsh gem a little easier in future. **Car ti ydi hwnna?** *Is that your car?*, **Gwaith pwy ydy o?** *Whose work is it?*

Swap out **gwely** for anything else that, upon realising you've woken up in someone else's house/room, finally kicks your brain in its backside and bashes the panic button. Swaps might include **cawod** (*shower*), **nenfwd** (*ceiling*), **cegin** (*kitchen*), **ymlacsedd / soffa** (*sofa*), or even **trôns** (*underwear*).

Mi fydda' i'n teimlo hwn 'fory hefyd

I'll be feeling this tomorrow too

Ah, the two-day hangover; the evil way your mid-20s body reminds you that you're not as good at handling your ale as well as you used to be!

What your 20+ brain *is* pretty good at, however, is recognising how the particle '**mi**' (which is often used to begin positive sentences in northern dialects of Welsh) can be dropped in standard Welsh. If you decide to drop it, you'll need to return **fydda'** to its unmutated form of **bydda'**.

If you've been to school in Wales, there's a decent chance you've heard the word '**teimlo**' (= *to feel*). The reason I bring it up here is because of how else it can be modified to mean different things; **teimlad** = *a feeling*, **teimladau** = *feelings*, **cydymdeimlad** = *sympathy* (literally, *joint-feeling*). You'll possibly hear this as '**timlo**' in southern dialects.

'**Fory** is simply a shortening of '**yfory**' (= *tomorrow*) and actually derives from the same root as the '*morrow*' part of the English term.

Well i fi beidio â tsecio'r banc!

I'd best not check the bank!

Perhaps you're aware of the adjective **gwell** (= *better*). Well (pun intended), it can be used in other ways too. **Well i fi/mi** = *I'd best, I'd better*. Simply adapt the '**i**' to talk about whosoever you like; w**ell i fi** = *I'd better*, **well i ni** = *we'd better*, **well iddyn nhw** = *they'd better*, **well i Owen** = *Owen had better*. You'll also see this phrase preceded by **basai'n** or **byddai'n** (both meaning '*it would be*'), but omission is acceptable in speech.

Peidio (literally; *to cease*) works better to form the negative here, although no one will spill their pint in disgust if you were to say '**ddim**' instead.

Tsecio, also written as **checio**, is a common way of expressing '*to check.*' The purists would be absolutely correct to encourage the use of '**gwirio**' (= *to verify*) here, where **gwir** means '*true.*'

The eagle-eyed amongst you may have spotted the letters **TYYW** on the picture for this sentence. This is just my hilarious way of subtly fashioning an opportunity to tell you that *a cash machine* (*an ATM*) are often known as '**t̲wll y̲n y̲ wa̲l**' in Welsh, translating as '*a hole in the wall.*'

Dw i byth yn yfed eto!

I'm never drinking again!

We've all uttered this one at some point in our lives, right? In my own case, numerous times!

As I mentioned how **byth** can be used in place of **ddim** to morph our sentences from '*not*' to '*never*,' so instead I'll offer a quick nod to **erioed**. **Erioed** also means *never* or *ever*, but it's used when talking about things that have happened. You'll likely see it coupled with **wedi** in perfect sentences; **wyt ti erioed wedi yfed fodca?** = *have you ever drunk vodka?* Unlike **byth**, however, **erioed** does not replace **ddim** in sentences.

Osgoa ben mawr, arhosa'n feddw!

Avoid a hangover, stay drunk!

The inclusion of endings, or suffixes, in Welsh can often throw up some strange looking words. Add the beauty of mutations into the mix and words that look like someone's drunkenly slapped their keyboard are created. Check out **hyfasid** for example... looks a bit bonkers, but actually means *'one had drunk'*.

The reason I raise the point of endings – and the peculiar terms they can yield – is because **osgoa** doesn't half look odd at first glance. In fact, it's simply the word **osgoi** (= *to avoid*) with the imperative **-a** ending added. Similarly, **aros** (= *to stay, to wait*) has also added a final **-a**... as well as a cheeky **-h-** in the middle.

Affixing **-a** in this way is the informal way of forming a command in Welsh; compare **arhoswch** and **arhosa**.

Finally, you've gotta love the Welsh word for *'a hangover'*... **pen mawr** (literally, *a large head*)!

CELTIC QUICK-FIX
ISBN: 9798585857645

CYMRAEG EFO FFRIND
ISBN: 9798531490421

CRACKING WELSH QUESTIONS
ISBN: 979-8774777815

WELSH WHILE YOU BONK
ISBN: 979-8422469628

THE FORGOTTEN CIRCLE
ISBN: 979804158080

THE SUREXIT SECRET
ISBN: 9798711837435

SAVING CAERWYDDNO
ISBN: 9798717273046

PARSNIPS AND OWLS
ISBN: 9798833259184

WELSH AND I
ISBN: 9798669438609

GEIRIADUR CYMRAEG-SESOTHO
ISBN: 9798717163989

DYDHLYVER KERNEWEK
ISBN: 9798544697275

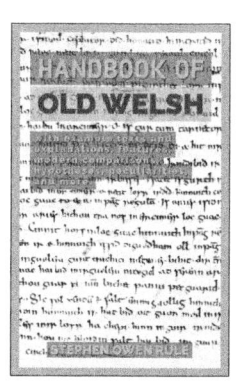

HANDBOOK OF OLD WELSH
ISBN: 9798444225370

Printed in Great Britain
by Amazon